D1127037

Solid or Liquid?

Anne Montgomery

Is it **solid** or **liquid**?

solid

liquid

solid

liquid

solid

liquid

solid

liquid

solid

liquid

solid

liquid

Is it solid or liquid?

Let's Do Science!

Can a solid become a liquid?
Try this!

What to Get

❏ clock or timer
❏ large ice cube
❏ small ice cube

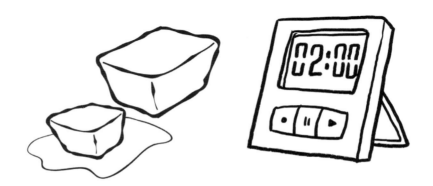

What to Do

1. Hold the small ice cube in your hand for a few minutes. What do you notice?

2. Hold the ice cube until it is gone. How long did it take?

3. Hold the large ice cube. How long does it take to melt? Switch hands if it gets too cold.

Glossary

liquid—can flow and be poured like water

solid—having a shape without a container

Index

Your Turn!

Watch something melt.
Use details to describe
what happens.

23

Consultants

Sally Creel, Ed.D.
Curriculum Consultant

Leann Iacuone, M.A.T., NBCT, ATC
Riverside Unified School District

Jill Tobin
California Teacher of the Year
Semi-Finalist
Burbank Unified School District

Publishing Credits

Conni Medina, M.A.Ed., *Managing Editor*
Lee Aucoin, *Creative Director*
Diana Kenney, M.A.Ed., NBCT, *Senior Editor*
Lynette Tanner, *Editor*
Lexa Hoang, *Designer*
Hillary Dunlap, *Photo Editor*
Rachelle Cracchiolo, M.S.Ed., *Publisher*

Image Credits: Cover & p.1 mparrilla/Getty Images/Flickr; p.23 Tony Cordoza/Getty Images; p.12 iStock; p.15 Osman Orsal/Reuters/Newscom; pp.18–19 (illustrations) J.J. Rudisill; all other images from Shutterstock.

Library of Congress Cataloging-in-Publication Data

Montgomery, Anne (Anne Diana), author.
  Solid or liquid? / Anne Montgomery.
    pages cm
  Summary: "It is time to learn about solids and liquids."—Provided by publisher.
  Audience: K to grade 3.
  Includes index.
  ISBN 978-1-4807-4527-8 (pbk.) —
  ISBN 978-1-4807-5136-1 (ebook)
1. Matter—Properties—Juvenile literature.
2. Solids—Juvenile literature.
3. Liquids—Juvenile literature. I. Title.
  QC173.36.M68 2015
  530.4—dc23
                              2014008926

Teacher Created Materials

5301 Oceanus Drive
Huntington Beach, CA 92649-1030
http://www.tcmpub.com
ISBN 978-1-4807-4527-8
© 2015 Teacher Created Materials, Inc.